How The Holy Trinity Communicates To Mankind

Dr. Aaron R. Jones

How the Holy Trinity
Communicates to Mankind

Copyright ©2002 Dr. Aaron R. Jones

Published by
Kingdom Publishing
Odenton, MD 21113
Printed in the USA

ISBN: 978-1-967006-03-8
Library of Congress Control Number: 2002093198

DEDICATION

To my Lord and Savior Jesus Christ who has blessed me with the talents, skills, and abilities to reach this point in my life.

Table of Contents

Foreword 1

Preface..3

Chapter 1: What Is The Holy Trinity?...9

Chapter 2: God The Father 13

Chapter 3: God The Son...19

Chapter 4: God The Spirit..26

Chapter 5: Displays Of The Holy Trinity 29

Chapter 6: Putting It All Together...34

FOREWORD

I feel quite privileged and highly honored to be asked by my colleague to write a foreword to his book, How the Holy Trinity Communicates to Mankind.

This book How the Holy Trinity Communicates to Mankind is a book for all: a book devoid of any denominational traits, but thoroughly Bible-based.

The language is the common man's colloquial language therefore to touch the heart of all, instead of limiting it to the highly educated and the theologically minded alone. I therefore commend the book to a wide readership

And concerning the main thesis, thrust and logic of the work, that is 'How the Holy Trinity Communicates to Mankind," I found the presentation quite simple and readily absorbable. It is foundational for those who have just been saved and desire to drink of the milk of the Gospel before graduating gradually to participate in consuming the flesh and bones of the Gospel and later devouring the bone of the Word of God. It is an effective presentation of how the

Scripture presents the Person of the Holy Trinity as an effective communicator to mankind.

This book sheds an illuminating light as an introduction of the Holy to new believers and Biblical students itching to be acquainted with the Holy Trinity.

Dr. Jacob Oguntomilade

PREFACE

To the Reader of this Book,

On August 5, 2001, God inspired me to write a book about the Holy Trinity. Nothing too long or so theological that an average person could not understand it. This is a very short book, but I believe it will speak to the heart of every believer and to help him or her better understand how the Godhead communicates to us daily. I believe no Christian should ever wonder, "What is really the truth?" Through this book the truth of the Holy Trinity will be revealed. The truths found in this book, will be able to be used in the believer's daily walk with God.

My prayer is that every reader will not only understand the Holy Trinity better but also seek in his or her daily life to come closer in relationship and communication with the Holy Trinity.

Dr. Aaron R. Jones

Chapter 1
WHAT IS THE HOLY TRINITY?

The Holy Trinity is one of the most misunderstood doctrines of the Bible. I believe without a proper understanding of the Holy Trinity; we will not have a clear understanding of our relationship or covenant with God. Our relationship with God must come first before all things. The Holy Trinity must come first in our daily walk with God.

What the believer must know, throughout the years, man has brought forth much controversy concerning the Holy Trinity: man has tried to make the Holy Trinity irrelevant for us today. To make this doctrine more complicated, there are many Bible scholars that believe that there is no such thing as Holy Trinity

The Holy Trinity is one essence manifested in three persons: God the Father, God the Son, and God the Spirit. Each person of the Holy Trinity has a distinct duty. God the Father is known as the creator, God the Son is known as the redeemer, and God the Spirit is known as the comforter. The original fall of mankind in Genesis 3 called for the work of the Holy Trinity.

Through that fall, we find the Everlasting Covenant, which was made in eternity, before time began in the counsels of the eternal Godhead.

Without the Everlasting Covenant, man would not have been able to return to God. The Everlasting Covenant simply reiterates the distinct duties of the Holy Trinity: God the Father is the originator, God the Son is the sacrifice, and God the Spirit is the sealer. The work of the Holy Trinity allows a sinful man, like me, the opportunity to see the creator one day.

One of the frequent questions that is asked, "How can three be one?" Every human being has a finite mind which means; it is limited; and you could never understand the Holy Trinity through limited capabilities. The whole essence of the Holy Trinity is infinite; you can never put limitations on something that is infinite. The Holy Trinity must be believed by faith, which God has given a measure to every man.

Romans 12:3 says, *"...God hath dealt to every man the measure of faith."* Many cults believe that the lack of the word Holy Trinity in the Bible gives good reasons not to believe it exists. The word Holy Trinity may not be spelled out in the Bible, but it is displayed throughout the New Testament. We will speak more on the display of the Holy Trinity in another chapter. A few natural points have been stated in order to help us understand the Holy Trinity better. The examples will never be the foundation for the Christian's belief in the Holy Trinity, but they are worth looking at to help clarify our comprehension of the three-in-one dynamic.

1. Our government is one with three distinctive sections— legislative, judicial, and executive.
2. Water is one and it comes in three forms— boiling, distilled, and frozen.
3. A triangle is one and it has three sides.

In the next three chapters, we will discuss briefly how the Holy Trinity communicates to the believer.

Chapter 2
GOD THE FATHER

God the Father is known as the Creator. It is understood by many scholars that God the Father played the biggest role in creation, based on Scriptures; however, we do know that Jesus and the Holy Trinity Spirit did play significant roles in creation. The two Scriptures that support this statement are Job 33:4, which says, *"The spirit of God hath made me, and the breath of the Almighty hath given me life."* And John 1:10, which says, *"He was in the world, and the world was made by him, and the world knew him* **(Jesus)** *not."* (emphasis added)

God the Father Communicates Order

God the Father communicates to mankind through creation. I believe Genesis 1 is the foundation of His communication to the believer. Genesis 1:2-3 says,

"And the earth was without form, and void; and darkness was upon the face of the deep. And the

Spirit of God moved upon the face of the waters. And God said, let there be light: and there was light."

One of the first things God the Father communicates to us is order. There was no form in the world; and God the Father saw that something needed to be done. God the Father called forth light. To begin the establishment of order on the earth, light needed to be brought into the darkness. God the Father used that light as the beginning tool for order on the earth.

Before every believer came to God, his/her life was without form or void and darkness filled it. No matter where you were born; how much money you had; what position you held at your job, or how together you felt, until the light of Jesus Christ filled your life you were in total darkness. To bring order into our lives, we needed the light of a Savior. This light is the beginning piece that's missing in our lives. It's what we need to lead us in the right direction.

If God the Father from the beginning is communicating order to us, then He could never be the creator of confusion.

This is why I Corinthians 14:33 says, *"For God is not the author of confusion…"* God the Father communicates order because He is a God of order and He wants us to have order in our lives. To have true order in our lives we need the Light of Jesus Christ.

God the Father Communicates Separation

God the Father is a God of separation. Genesis 1:4 says, *"And God saw the light, that it was good: God divided the light from darkness."* We know that throughout Scripture, light is symbolic of Jesus Christ. Scripture makes several references or contrast to light and darkness. John 8:12 says, Jesus said to the people, *"I am the light of the world. If you follow me, you won't be stumbling through the darkness, because you will have the light that leads to life."* We also know that darkness has been symbolic of Satan. Ephesians 6:12 says, *"For we wrestle not against flesh and blood, but against principalities, against power, against the rulers of the darkness of this world…"*. John 1:5 says, *"And the light shineth in darkness; and the darkness comprehended not."*

When God the Father communicates separation, He lets us know that from the beginning that light and darkness were not meant to be together. The reason for God the Father sending His only begotten Son was so that darkness in our lives could be separated from us. My friend, whatever darkness that is in your life, it is time to separate from it. Your darkness can be adultery, fornication, lying, cheating, stealing, or gossiping, and the list can go on. God the Father saw that the light was good, then He separated the light from darkness.

God the Father Communicates Time and Season

How do I know what day, month, year, or season it is? When did all this begin? God the Father communicates to us time. Genesis 1:14 says, *"And God said, Let there be lights in the firmament of the heaven to divide the day from the night: and let them be for sign, and for season, and for days and for years."* From the beginning of time, God the Father placed a time system in place so that we could tell when summer or winter was here. We can tell what day it is or what month is coming up next. Although God the Father created time,

He is not a part of time. Psalm 90:2 says, *"Before the mountains were brought forth, or ever thou hadst formed the earth and the world, even from everlasting to everlasting, thou art God."*

God is an infinite being which cannot be ruled by time, neither can His will for our lives. When God deals with us, He steps into time. When God the Father placed separation in the days, years, and seasons, He communicates to us that certain events will take place in different times of the year. Every event that takes place has it own season, there is a season to be hot and there is a season to be cold.

There are many events we as believers want to take place in our lives right now, but it just may not be the season for it. God operates in his absolute will, I believe there is no permissive will with God. The permissive will is man's will. One of the goals of every believer is to understand God's absolute will for his/her life; and know that it will be manifested in their seasons. If not, one will always miss the divine plans ordered by God. Ecclesiastes 3:1 says, *"To every thing there is a season, and a time to every purpose under the sun."*

The understanding of order, separation, time and seasons are three basic truths that the believer needs to understand to be able to comprehend God the Father as the Creator. I believe that these basic truths are keys to the spiritual growth of every believer.

In the next chapter, we will discuss what God the Son communicates to us. When the world was lost in sin, God the Father sent His Son. John 3:16 says, *"For God so loved the world, that he gave his only begotten Son, that whosoever believeth in him shall not perish, but have eternal life."*

Chapter 3
GOD THE SON

There remains much controversy over the second person of the Holy Trinity. One might ask the question, what is the argument? Many people do not have a problem with Jesus Christ being the Son of God; most religions embrace the notion. The problem arises, however, when we say that Jesus Christ is also God. What do you tell a person who asks the question, "If Jesus died on the cross, how can he be God?

In this chapter, I want to do two things: first, express what God the Son communicates to us. Second, explain how Jesus can be God and man at the same time. Let's look at the first passage of Scripture.

Philippians 2:6-8 reads,

"Who being in the form of God, thought it not robbery to be equal with God: But made himself of no reputation, and took upon him the form of a servant, and was made in the likeness of men: And being found in fashion as a man, he humbled

himself and became obedient unto death, even the death of the cross."

Here we find God the Son communicating two awesome Christian responsibilities, obedience and humility. What makes this so awesome is the fact that Jesus is God and man.

God the Son Communicates His Divinity

In verse six, it tells us that Jesus thought it was not robbery to be equal with God. Why? Because Jesus was God. Jesus felt he wasn't taking anything from God that did not belong to Him. Scriptures back Jesus' reasoning. John 17:5 says, *"And now, O Father glorify thou me with thine own self the glory which I had with thee before the world was."* John 1:1 says, *"In the beginning was the Word, and the Word was with God, and the Word was God."*

These verses identify Jesus being with God, as well as being God from the beginning of time. Understanding that Jesus is God plays an important role in comprehending what God the Son communicates to us in Philippians 2: 6-8 which says,

"Who, being in the form of God, thought it not robbery to be equal with God: But made himself of no reputation, and took upon him the form of a servant, and was made in the likeness of men: And being found in fashion as a man, he humbled himself, and became obedient unto death, even the death of the cross."

God the Son Communicates Humility

In verse seven, God the Son communicates humility; remember Jesus is God. When Jesus took on the form of a servant, He voluntarily laid His divinity to the side and exemplified humility. The question you may be asking yourself is "how could Jesus lay aside His divinity?" Just as a man who takes his coat off and lays its own a chair, the coat doesn't cease from being his possession. Jesus laid down his divinity for you and me. Then in verse eight, Jesus displays the ultimate example of humility by dying on the cross so that you and I may have eternal life.

God the Son had to lay aside something for redemption to come to mankind. Humility must be a by-product of every believer's life. The

Word of God tells us that God gives grace to the humble. Jesus dying on the cross communicates the perfect example of humility and obedience.

What God the Son communicates to us is we must be willing to give up and lay aside our status, agenda, or our life so that one may come to the saving knowledge of Jesus Christ.

God the Son Communicates Obedience

God the Son in other places of Scripture communicates obedience. John 6:38 reads, *"For I came down from heaven, not to do mine own will, but the will of him that sent me."* God the Son gives true understanding of obedience. Obedience is not only obeying, but it is a decision to place your will to the side, so that the will of God might be fulfilled. Until we as believers learn how to allow God's will to be first in our lives; true obedience will not take place in our walk with God.

God the Son Communicates Surrendering Man's Will

God the Son communicates the perfect example of the surrendering of man's will. Matthew 26:39

says, *"...O my Father, if it be possible, let this cup pass from me: Nevertheless not as I will, but as thy will."* Remembering Jesus was 100% human, he struggled with his will against the will of the Father. The cup that Jesus had to drink was not His sins, but the sins of the world. We all struggle against the will of God for our lives. We must come to a point as Jesus did where the will of the Father must be done. We must understand the will of the Father always has the bigger picture in mind. The surrendering of your will is for the salvation of many.

Just think for a moment, what if Jesus did not surrender his will in Gethsemane? Our will, more often than not, is very narrow and has only our own interests at heart. The context of Scripture lets us know that Jesus was exceedingly sorrowful, because He was about to face the cross; yet it was for our redemption, therefore he submitted His will to God's plan. What are you placing before God's will? Could it possibly be costing someone his or her life?

So, in this chapter we have discussed God the Son communicating divinity, humility, obedience, and the surrendering of man's will. Truthfully, the last three characteristics go hand-in-hand and without them working in your life, true submission to God cannot be obtained.

In the next chapter, we will look at the communication of God the Spirit. John 16:7 says, *"Nevertheless I tell you the truth; it is expedient for you that I go away: for if I go not away, the Comforter will not come unto you: but if I depart, I will send him unto you."* Expedient in the Greek literally means "profitable." In Chapter four, we will see what makes Jesus leaving the earth and sending God the Spirit profitable to the believer.

Chapter 4
GOD THE HOLY SPIRIT

God the Spirit is the third person of the Holy Trinity. God the Spirit is the connecting person we need to accomplish all that has been communicated by God the Father and God the Son.

God the Spirit Communicates He is Our Teacher and Brings Remembrance

John 14:26 reads, *"But the Comforter which is the Holy Ghost, whom the Father will send in my name, he shall teach you all things, and bring all things to your remembrance whatsoever I have said unto you."*

What God the Spirit is communicating to the believer is not only that He is our teacher, but also that He is the person who brings all things back to our remembrance. Most believers do not realize that God the Spirit is our ultimate teacher. The Scripture say, *"Teach you all things."* We must develop a prayer life that requests the teaching of the Spirit in all the activities we encounter. You see, all that we do should be for the glory of God and we need the teaching of God the Spirit to fulfill that responsibility. God the Spirit is the primary teacher of the Word of God. Without the Spirit, there is no divine interpretation of the Word.

When we are going through the trial of life or when we need a word for the defense of the gospel, God the Spirit is the person who brings back the Word of God to help us. I have a question for you: Can God the Spirit bring to remembrance something that has never been placed in you? To answer that question, I believe for the Spirit to bring anything back to our remembrance, something must be there first.

What I am saying is we must invest quality time in the Word and with our God, so that our spirit can be saturated with the Word. So when the enemy comes against me, God the Spirit can bring back to mind that which I have meditated on. As well as when we face the trials of life, the Spirit will bring a continuous flow of the Word to our remembrance to encourage and uplift us.

God the Spirit Communicates He is Our Guide

John 16:13 says, *"Howbeit when he, the Spirit of truth, is come, he will guide you into all truth: for he shall not speak of himself: but whatsoever he shall hear, that shall he speak: and he will show you things to come."*

One of the reasons Scripture tells us to walk not after the flesh, but after the Spirit, is because God the Spirit is our guide into all truth. We can never go wrong by listening to the Spirit.

Every day, we must decide whether to walk after the flesh or walk after the Spirit. As I stated earlier, God always sees the bigger picture for our lives; so, we must put our trust in Him.

Never dismiss when the Spirit instructs you in a situation or circumstance. Without God the Spirit, you are bound to end up in trouble. John 16:13, gives us a promise if we walk after the Spirit we will be guided into truth. This does not mean every step will be trial or tribulation free, but that every step will be in the will of God.

In this chapter, we have discussed God the Spirit communicating to us, He is our teacher, guide, and the person who brings things to our remembrance. Without God the Spirit, you will find yourself walking in circles instead of walking with God.

Chapter 5
DISPLAYS OF THE HOLY TRINITY IN SCRIPTURE

In this chapter, we will discuss briefly three Scripture references where the Holy Trinity is being displayed in the New Testament.

The Holy Trinity Involved in Our Salvation

I Peter 1:2 reads, *"Elect according to the foreknowledge of God the Father, through sanctification of the Spirit, unto obedience and sprinkling of the blood of Jesus Christ..."*

What makes this Scripture so valuable? It identifies the distinct duty of each person of the Holy Trinity. This verse tells how we received our salvation. God the Father called us out according to His foreknowledge of how we would respond to Him. Our callings are not based on anything within us. The will of God is based on His foreknowledge of all things.

Remember God always sees the bigger picture. One of the roles of God the Spirit that we did not talk about is He working sanctification through believers. God the Spirit is separating us for the work of the ministry. Sanctification is a process that is intended not to cease, we are to work daily at separating ourselves from things that are not godly.

In chapter 3, we talked about Jesus humbling Himself and dying on the cross. We talked about the blood that He shed brought forth the remission of our sins. This blood was symbolic of the blood that the Old Testament priest sprinkled on the altars in the Holiest of Holies once a year to cover the sins of the people.

The Holy Trinity Involved in Baptism

Matthew 3:16, 17 says, *"And Jesus, when he was baptized, went up straightway out of the water: and, lo, the heavens were opened unto him, and he saw the Spirit of God descending like a dove, and lighting upon him. And lo a voice from heaven, saying, this is my beloved Son, in whom I am well pleased."*

Here we find God the Father testifying of God the Son. God the Son is showing forth humility by being baptized by John the Baptist. Many ask the question, why do we have to get baptized? One of the main reasons we get baptized is to identify with Christ and His humility. Not only does God the Father speak of God the Son, but God the Spirit glorifies and anoints Him while He is on earth. This was the opportunity for Jesus' ministry to be elevated and the Holy Trinity was on one accord. We, the body of Christ, need to know how to display unity so the work of God can be completed.

The Holy Trinity Involved in Grace, Love, and Communion

II Corinthians 13:14 says, *"The grace of the Lord Jesus Christ, and the love of God, and the communion of the Holy Ghost, be with you."* In the letters Paul wrote to the church of Corinth, he dealt with many problems such as division and disorder. Paul understood that it would take the triune God to help them overcome these problems that were prevalent in the church.

So, as Paul closes out this letter by pronouncing blessings upon the church through the Godhead.

Without grace, love, and communion, there is no church. These three powerful elements come from the Holy Trinity, but they must be displayed one to another.

Chapter 6
PUTTING IT ALL TOGETHER

As we have stated earlier, the Holy Trinity is one essence manifested in three persons. These three persons have very distinct roles and jobs in the believer's life. Through Scriptures, we find the Holy Trinity was always on one accord. When it was time to speak of another, they did. Being one should always display unity. Understanding the reason, we have intimate relationship with God is because of the Holy Trinity; outside of the Holy Trinity, there is no intimate relationship. Each person of the Holy Trinity played a unique role in our salvation.

We said, God the Father communicates order, separation, and time. God the Son communicates divinity, humility, obedience, and the surrendering of man's will. God the Spirit communicates as our teacher, guide, and brings all things back to our remembrance. My friend, we have only scratched the surface of how the Holy Trinity communicates to us; but I believe this is a good start for someone who has no clue about the Holy Trinity. What we have discussed are key elements needed for the believer to walk in oneness with God. For us to mature correctly as Christians, we need to know what the Holy Trinity is saying to us.

The question is asked, "Why are we here?" One of the most powerful commandments of God is found in Matthew 28:19 which reads, *"Go ye therefore, and teach all nations, baptizing them in the name of the Father, and of the Son, and of the Holy Ghost."* Here we are told to witness to the world in the name of the Holy Trinity. We are here to evangelize the world. Though, we all are not called to be Evangelists, we are called to evangelize. We will need the work of the Holy Trinity to fulfill the call that is on every believer's life.

God the Father, God the Son, and God the Spirit make up the Holy Trinity and these three are one God. I John 5:7 says, *"For there are three that bear record in heaven, the Father, the Word (Son), and the Holy Ghost: and these three are one."*

Role of the Holy Trinity

God the Father	God the Son	God the Holy Spirit
Designer of the Redemptive Program of Mankind	Made provision by His Death, Resurrection, and Glorification for the Redemptive Program for Mankind	Proved and empowered the execution of the Redemptive Program for Mankind
Creator	Redeemer	Comforter
The Originator	The Sacrifice	The Sanctifier
Communicates: • Order • Separation of Ethnic Races • Times and Seasons Love	Communicates: • His Divinity • Humility • Obedience • Surrendering of Man's Will to God's Will • Grace	Communicates: • His role as a Teacher and He who brings remembrance • Illuminator of the Word • Provider of Interpretation • His role as a guide • Communion and Fellowship